AR WIL S

My Favorite Photos from "The Natural State"

TIM ERNST

CLOUDLAND.NET PUBLISHING
CAVE MOUNTAIN, ARKANSAS

Library of Congress Control Number : 2002093176
ISBN 1–882906–47–0

Book designed by Tim Ernst
Other production team members:
Pam Ernst, John Coghlan, Norma Senyard, and Glenn Wheeler

All the photographs in this book are
available as custom-printed images.
Autographed, personalized copies of this book
and all other books by Tim Ernst are available as well.
To order, contact the author direct:

Tim Ernst
CLOUDLAND.NET
HC 33, BOX 50–A
Pettigrew, AR 72752
800–838–HIKE (4453)
E-mail: TimErnst@TimErnst.com
or visit our Web site:
www.Cloudland.net

Coneflowers, (double exposure blur), Leatherwood Wilderness, Ozark National Forest

Introduction

Welcome to the greatest hits of Arkansas! Every image in this collection is a favorite of mine, and was taken during the first 30 years of my photography career. These are the scenes that you would find hanging on the walls of our cabin, if we had the room. Many of them have been published in other books or calendars of mine, or in the many dozens of publications that have used my work over the years (including 16 that were magazine or book covers).

More than 50 of these images are brand new, and have never seen the light of day. In fact, while digging through more than a million photographs in my files to make the selections for this book, I discovered images that I never even knew I had! It was really quite easy picking out pictures to go into the book, but after the first edit I discovered that I had selected way too many, and had to cut out more than 50. Talk about having to pick between your favorite children! What remains are the cream of the crop, and I present them here for your enjoyment.

Arkansas has always been my home, and while I have photographed extensively in other wild areas of the country (in 44 states so far), I always return to the most beautiful place on earth, "The Natural State." I live in a log cabin called Cloudland at the edge of the Buffalo River Wilderness with my wife and partner Pam, and our daughter Amber. The wilderness is as close as our backyard, and you will see many images taken within sight of our cabin. Pam had a great deal to do with the final image selection, and Amber even helped out too.

Each new season brings displays of great beauty and targets for my camera. While I explore many new places throughout the year, I will also return to the same ones over and over again, always searching for a new angle, a better way to capture the "feel" of the place, or more dramatic light or color. One thing that I never tire of is seeing a spectacular scene for the very first time. More than once I have been stopped in my tracks, my breath taken away, and have been brought to tears by a scene that was simply too beautiful to capture on film. Sometimes you just have to sit there in awe. Arkansas really is an incredible place, one of the natural wonders of the world.

The images in this book are not arranged in any particular order, and there are no chapters. I hope that you will find them easy to look through, with one photograph blending into the next like a slide program as you turn the pages. All of the images have some caption information, and there are a few stories here and there that illustrate something about a particular photo. For you shutterbugs, there is a list of camera gear and photo discussion in the back of the book.

As you go through this book it is my hope that you will not only enjoy the images, but will also come to appreciate the natural beauty that we have here in Arkansas. Much of that beauty is fragile and unprotected, and it will take constant vigilance on our part to keep our state wild and free for the many generations that follow. With that, I give you my photo album. Enjoy!

Tim Ernst

Whitaker Creek, Upper Buffalo Wilderness, Ozark National Forest

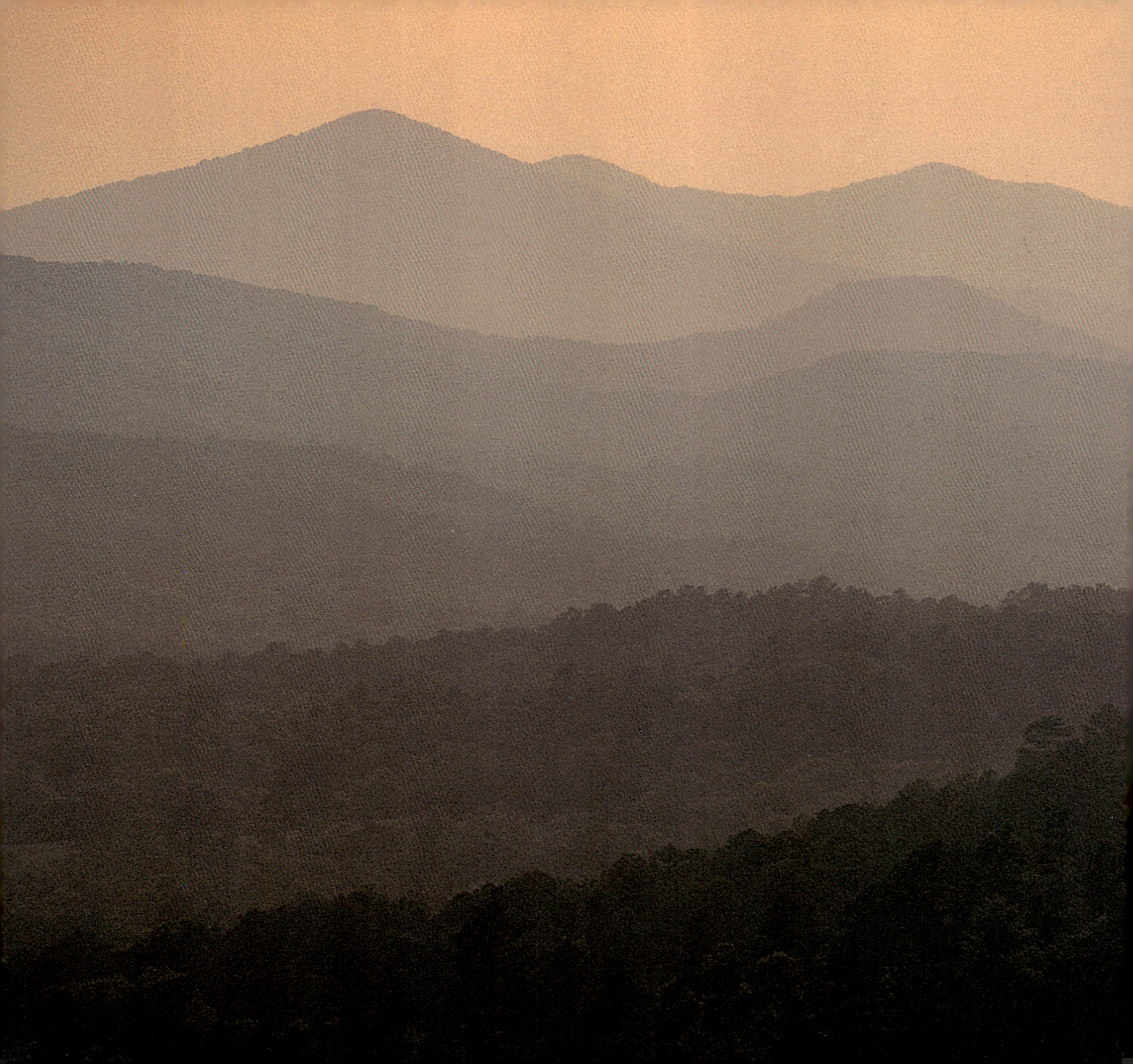

"Leaf-fall" at Cloudland

When conditions are just right, a large percentage of the colorful fall leaves will turn loose and rain down in a matter of minutes. I call this event "leaf-fall." It doesn't happen very often—not even every year— but I look forward to it and treasure each moment when I am able to be out in the woods at the right time. I've even been known to lie down in the forest and let the leaves fall where they may, often covering me completely up.

*Many people ask if I placed the leaves on the sandstone boulder in this picture. Heck no! As a matter of fact, the leaves were raining down so fast that I had to stop several times and **remove** the many leaves that were piling up and carpeting the rock.*

Leaf-fall is truly a magical time in the forest, and I highly recommend spending time in the fall to see if you can catch it happening. It is a beautiful display of color, movement, and wilderness music.

Our cabin at Cloudland is surrounded by many maple trees, and they put on quite a display in late October. Early mornings often bring fog in, creating an ideal backdrop for fall color photography.

This image was shot using a wide-angle lens and stopped down all the way for maximum depth of field.

◄ Caney Creek Wilderness, Ouachita National Forest

Indian Pipe, East Fork Wilderness, Ozark National Forest

This is actually a wildflower, but it has no green chlorophyll, which accounts for the odd coloration. These flowers are unable to produce their own food, so they must feed on nutrients from decaying organic material in the soil. I rarely see them, but always marvel at how unusual they are. If you look real close, you can see the flowers. Another one of Momma Nature's great beauties!

Kings River Falls, Kings River Natural Area

Fly fisherman on Big Piney Creek, Ozark National Forest

◄ Western daisies and coreopsis, limestone glade, Buffalo National River

Maple leaf and early season snow, Buffalo National River

We had a rare October snow one year while I was out chasing fall color. The sky cleared overnight and the bright sun came up early. The snow must have liked this lone maple leaf because it was holding onto it for dear life, not allowing it to blow away. I had to lie down on my belly to get low enough to take this picture.

Sandstone blocks, Busby Hollow, Henson Creek drainage, Newton County

Young maple trees in the fog, Ozarks

◄ Hemmed-In Hollow Falls and winter sun, Ponca Wilderness, Buffalo National River

Hawksbill Crag in the mist,
Upper Buffalo Wilderness, Ozark National Forest

It was more than twenty years ago when I took my first photograph of Hawksbill Crag. It continues to be a favorite subject of mine and I remain awed by the incredible beauty that I find with each visit.

This image is my latest attempt to capture the drama and scenic quality of the Crag. It was taken early one September morning specifically for the cover of the book <u>The Search For Haley</u>*. My daughter, Amber, was the model (age eight at the time), and she did a great job of holding still in the chilly morning air while I fired off shot after shot.*

The fog banks were moving around rapidly, often covering up the background entirely, and even the Crag itself disappeared a time or two. The scene changed constantly, and I worked frantically to get something that would work for the book cover—the book was going to press later in the week and this was my last chance to get it right. And then just as the fog bank retreated to the perfect location, I ran out of film. Luckily, I was able to get three good images before the end—this shot was the very last frame! Amber ran back up the hill just in time to catch the bus to school and retain her "perfect attendance" record.

I can't explain exactly why, but this photo is perhaps my favorite photograph of all time, certainly one of the top two or three that I have ever taken.

◄ Coreopsis, larkspur, & daisy fleabane, Arkansas River Valley

Spiderwort, Caney Creek Wilderness, Ouachita National Forest

Cinnamon ferns along the Ouachita Trail, Ouachita National Forest (poster available)

Dogwood leaves and beech tree, Ozarks

◄ Backwater swamp, morning light, Cadron River drainage

Fire pink and moss, Caney Creek Wilderness, Ouachita National Forest

The "pink" in the name comes from the fact that the tips of these striking wildflowers resemble pinking shears.

➤ Sycamore tree and winter sky, Leatherwood Wilderness, Ozark National Forest

McNamara Spring, Upper Buffalo Wilderness, Buffalo National River

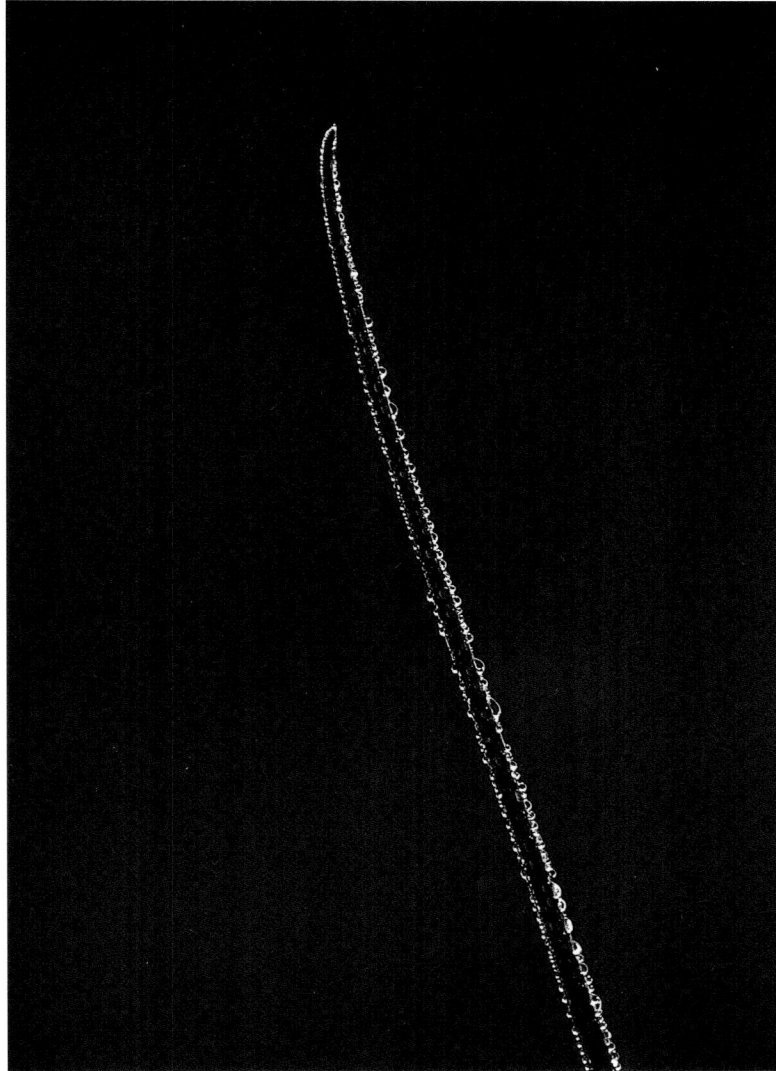

Dew drops on wild onion, Little Red River Valley

◄   William McNamara is a terrific watercolor artist. He has spent many years wandering around in the Buffalo River wilderness painting the scenes that he comes to know intimately. He told me one time that this particular spring did not exist twenty years ago. The rock layers must have shifted below the surface and diverted water from nearby Dug Hollow, producing this lush cascade down the hillside. I took the liberty of naming the spring after its most famous admirer.

Western daisies and weathered cedar, Buffalo National River

Purple is my daughter's favorite color, so these little wildflowers remind me of her. They are located in a wet limestone glade near the banks of the middle part of the Buffalo River.

When I sat down to write about this photo, she said that I should talk about how the cedar log got there (she was sitting in my lap while I wrote this). That's a good question. I come across unique and interesting pieces of weathered wood all the time in the forest, and always wonder what their history is.

I can imagine this bit of wood was once part of a large, majestic cedar that grew on top of a tall bluff, and leaned out over the river, far upstream. Pioneers, and even Native Americans, gazed up at the tree when they floated by. As the tree weathered and got older, a mighty storm passed through and knocked it over, sending it crashing down, coming to rest at the edge of the river. In years to come floods washed the tree downstream, until finally one year a massive flood carried the wood, now broken into many pieces, high up on the bank, and it came to rest in the glade where it sits today. Amber thinks that a little girl just like her used to sit on the log and do her homework—well, perhaps maybe think about boys and stuff. As time went on, wildflowers took a liking to the log and grew up all around it. Then one day, a photographer spent an hour standing over the log, patiently waiting for the wind to die down so that the flowers would be still and sharp in the photo. Click. Click. Here is your picture!

◄ Water-worn sandstone pebbles along the banks of the Buffalo River

Tunnel Cave Falls (Arkansas Cave), ferns, Indian Creek, Buffalo National River

◄ Maple forest in full fall dress, Ozark National Forest

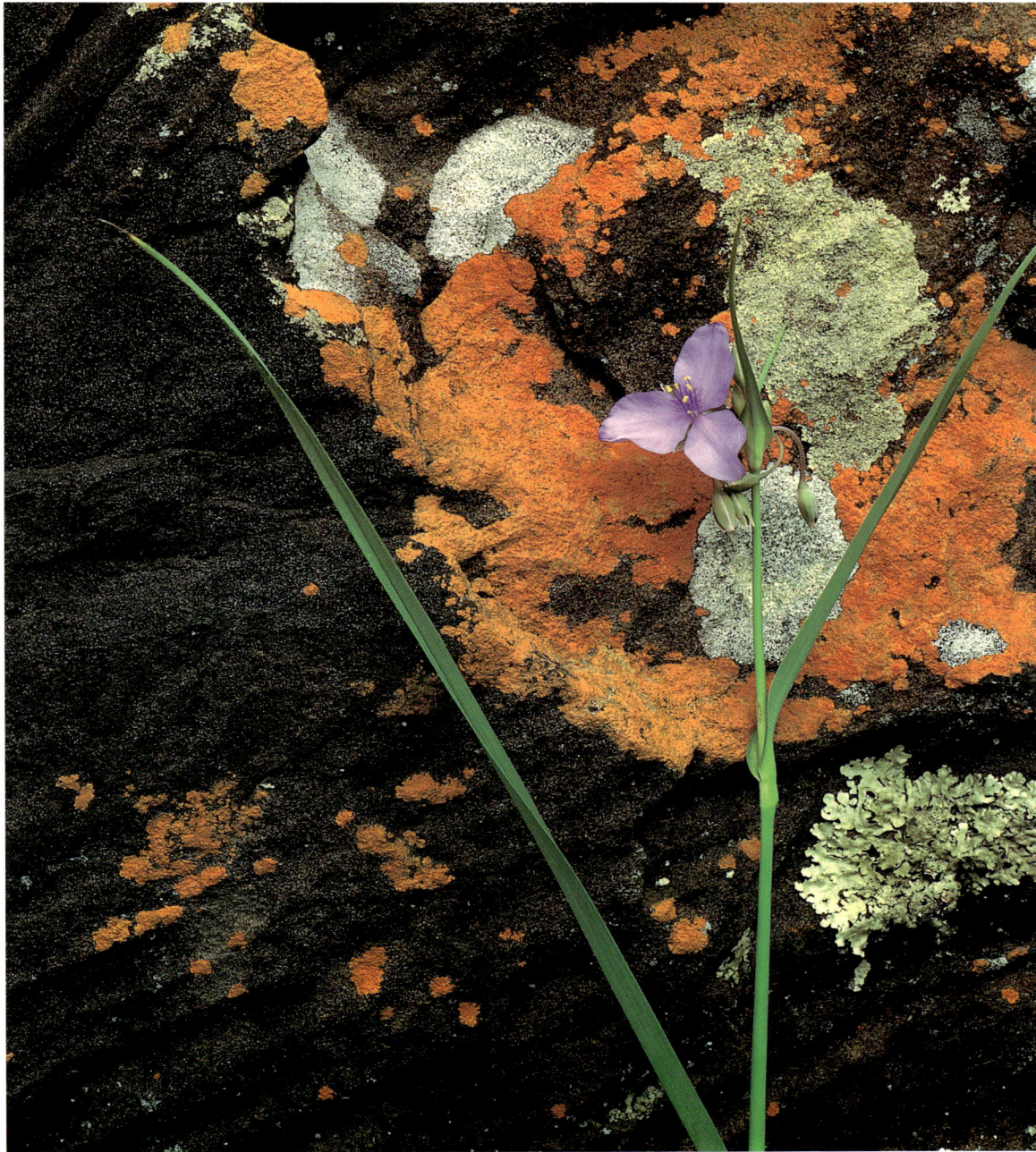

Spiderwort and lichen rock, Petit Jean State Park

◄ Cypress trees at low water, White River National Wildlife Refuge

Dogwood and maple leaves, dogwood berries, and moss, Boxley Valley, Buffalo National River

Alum Cove Natural Bridge at sunrise, Ozark National Forest

This is a huge natural stone bridge, large enough that they used to drive vehicles across it. It is located in the Alum Cove Scenic Area, a neat little place that has many places to explore. I was down under this giant arch one morning looking for wildflowers to photograph when I "felt" something peering at me over my shoulder. I turned around and saw the sun beaming through the trees—I had no idea you could watch the sunrise from UNDER this natural bridge!

Redbud and mist, near Ponca

Pearly Spring, Boxley Valley, Buffalo National River

The view from our back deck at Cloudland, Upper Buffalo Wilderness, Ozark National Forest

This is the scene that we wake up to nearly every morning at our log cabin home we call Cloudland (named that for obvious reasons). The clouds are not always there, but the hills usually are, unless the clouds have risen and covered them up. This part of Arkansas has not only the purest air in the state, but also a quality of light that I have not seen anyplace else. Mornings are especially nice, as sunlight spills into the valleys and wakes everything up.

The Buffalo River is 700 feet down there below the clouds, and we can hear it singing all day long. We hear hoot owls and coyotes and the drumming of woodpeckers echoing across the wilderness, too. I have been exploring this area for many years now, yet have barely scratched the surface. I plan to grow old poking around under those clouds, and will continue to take pictures and share it all with you as long as I can.

◄ Baby blue-eyes, Arkansas River Valley (poster available)

Purple coneflower (double exposure blur), Leatherwood Wilderness, Ozark National Forest

Mule Trail Falls and ferns, Upper Buffalo Wilderness Area, Ozark National Forest

48

Serviceberry or "Popcorn" tree, Ozark National Forest

Serviceberry trees (locals call them "sarvis") are usually the first trees to bloom in spring, and many people mistake them for dogwoods. I have heard that in the old days the winter ground was often frozen, and it was tough to dig graves by hand. When these trees bloomed, it was a sign that the ground had thawed, and they could have a "service" for the dead—hence the name serviceberry. I call them "popcorn" trees because they look like someone glued a bunch of popcorn to the limbs.

➤ *To get to the spot to take this picture you have to crawl out onto a narrow fin of rock, with your feet dangling out there in space, hundreds of feet above the river. One wrong move and you die. This image once appeared in three national magazines in the same month.*

Roark Bluff and Buffalo River, Buffalo National River (poster available)

Red maple, Beaver Lake State Park

Fall leaves often look best if you can backlight them—all of the color and detail of the leaves will come shining through.

Hardwoods and pines in November, Caney Creek Wilderness, Ouachita National Forest

I love the contrast between the pines and hardwoods in the Ouachitas, especially in the fall. This shot was taken from the same viewpoint as the one on pages 6–7. The changing seasons and times of day produce many different moods.

Richland Creek and smooth sandstone boulders, Richland Wilderness, Ozark National Forest (poster available)

≺ Wild plum and redbud (double exposure blur) Ozark National Forest

Dew drop, sumac leaf, Lake Ft. Smith State Park

This single drop of dew caught my attention early one morning more than twenty years ago, and taught me a lesson that has become a fiber of my being. I think we all hunt for the grand vistas in life. We want bigger, faster, better, more expensive, the whole nine yards in an instant. Yet, if we will slow down and take a look at the details of our surroundings, and of our lives, I think we will see and enjoy and gain much more.

A single drop of dew. It forces you to focus tightly, to cut out the rest of the world, to concentrate on one detail at a time, and to give it your all. I took pictures of many things that day, but this lonely and lovely dew drop has survived the test of time, and even today, after I have seen the photo thousands of times, I still stop when I am turning the pages and pause for a few moments to admire the view.

This photo was taken with a macro lens, my favorite lens of choice on rainy days. If you look real close into the drop of dew, you can see a miniature vista— the sky, a large tree, and a tripod with a young photographer standing behind it—all of us upside down.

Next time you are out in the forest, look around you and see how many dew drops you can see, and what is reflected in them.

◄ A January snowstorm blankets the Upper Buffalo Wilderness, Ozark National Forest

58

Maple leaves in springtime, Ozarks

➤ Pre-dawn, Lake Fayetteville

A rare sight in Arkansas—fall color and water! Buffalo River, Ozark National Forest

Alum Cove Scenic Area, Ozark National Forest

62

Hang on tight Billy! Hawksbill Crag, Upper Buffalo Wilderness, Ozark National Forest. He lived.

Mayapple forest and morning fog, Ozarks

One of the best ways to photograph mayapples is to get down on the ground with a wide-angle lens. Get in real close and stop the lens all the way down so that everything is in focus. Damp, foggy days are best. Right after I shot this picture my dog, Aspen, ran through the scene and trampled this flower.

64

Hemmed-In Hollow Falls, Ponca Wilderness, Buffalo National River

Wild rose, Buffalo River Wilderness

Yellow lady slipper orchid, Buffalo River Wilderness

Whenever I come across a wild orchid in the forest I have to stop, sit down, and admire its incredible beauty. They simply take my breath away every time.

I came across this particular orchid one day while out chasing waterfalls. There was no flower then, only the broad, unmistakable leaves. I returned to her every several days, watching, waiting, hoping she would produce a flower. After several weeks, a flower began to appear, and I found myself spending more and more time with her.

There is a picture book in my library by the famous photographer Bert Stern. It is called __The Last Sitting__, and is filled with photographs he took one evening of Marilyn Monroe—they ended up being the last series of photographs ever taken of her. Bert was infatuated with Marilyn (as she was with the camera), shot hundreds of pictures of her, and recorded raw Marilyn at her best during his evening of love-making through the camera.

This orchid became my Marilyn, and on the day she grew into perfection, I went into the forest to dance with a goddess. As the golden glow of the setting sun softly lit her up, I shot roll after roll of film—I wanted to make SURE I did her justice! This simple image is no doubt one of my all-time favorites.

◄ October reflections in the Mulberry River, Ozark National Forest

Sunrise from Petit Jean State Park

There is a great viewpoint at the far end of this popular park where you can see the sun rise above the Arkansas River (it's called Petit Jean's Grave, but there really isn't a grave). I climbed down into some of the rock formations there and found this scene. I was down low, stretched out on my belly, and had to work fast without a tripod in order to get the sun peeking out from under the rock. You can't believe how quickly the sun will move when you are trying to line it up against a solid object like this!

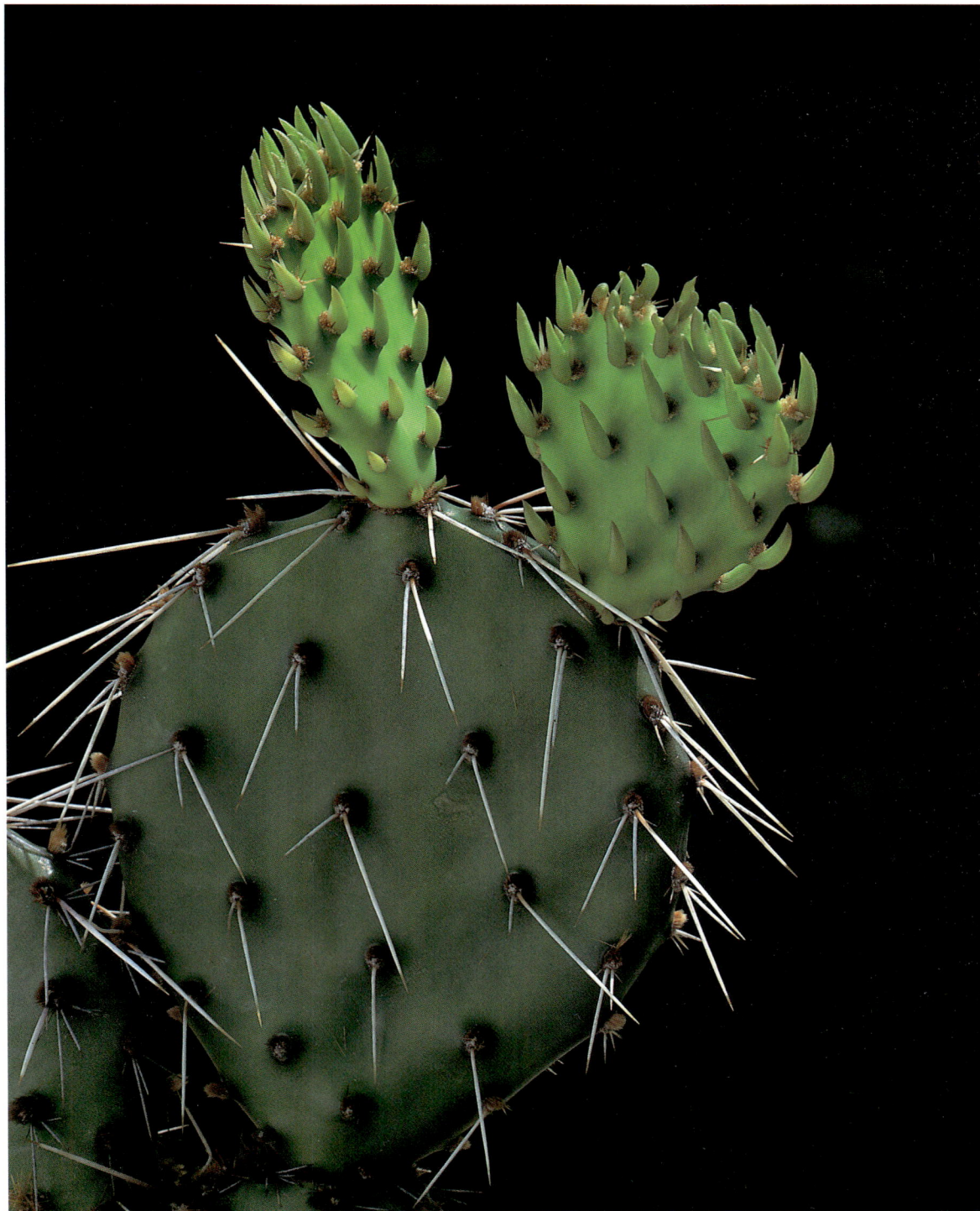

Prickly pear cactus, Sylamore Creek area, Ozark National Forest

Fall scene, Little Missouri River, Ouachita National Forest (poster available)

Spring scene, Little Missouri River, Ouachita National Forest

Daffodils and ice, Buffalo River Wilderness

One way to find old pioneer homesites is to wander around in the forest in early spring. If you come across some daffodils in bloom, chances are they were planted around an old log cabin that has long since disappeared. Some of these flowers are 50 to 75 years old or more, hardy enough to survive the test of time, and to shrug off the occasional ice storm that meets them unexpectedly. Once the ice melted, the flowers above continued to bloom for another two or three weeks.

Crested iris, Hilary Hollow, Ouachita Trail, Ouachita National Forest

Arkansas Cave Falls (Tunnel Cave Falls), Indian Creek, Ponca Wilderness, Buffalo National River

Sandstone boulder, weathered root, Hurricane Creek Wilderness, Ozark National Forest

View from Flatside Pinnacle, Ouachita Trail, Ouachita National Forest

This photograph conveys exactly the way I feel many times when I reach the top of a mountain—I can see FAR and WIDE! It was taken with a fish-eye lens, and while this lens gives a view that is actually much wider than humans can see in a single look, it does show the panorama that is recorded in our minds.

This viewpoint is located within an hour's drive from Little Rock. It is a short, but steep, hike from the trailhead up to the top. It looks out over the Flatside Wilderness, and is one of the best places to watch the sunset in the Ouachitas. Be sure to bring your fish-eyes with you!

◄ Dogwoods and redbud, Richland Creek Wilderness, Ozark National Forest (poster available)

Wild cherry leaves, cedar berries, club moss, Lower Buffalo Wilderness, Buffalo National River

➤ *This was the first waterfall that I ever named. I called it "Copperhead" falls because there was a copperhead snake coiled up next to my camera bag while I was taking this photo. He was very nice and never caused any trouble. While working on my Arkansas Waterfalls Guidebook, I had to give names to more than 60 previously unnamed waterfalls—that's just part of the job!*

Copperhead Falls on Indian Creek, Ponca Wilderness, Buffalo National River (poster available)

January snowstorm, Hawksbill Crag, Upper Buffalo Wilderness, Ozark National Forest

Both of these photographs were kind of taken at the same place. The snow scene above was shot looking AT Hawksbill Crag, and the fall scene to the right was taken FROM the Crag looking over towards the other camera location. I find myself returning to the same locations over and over again at different times of the year and often find many new scenes to photograph.

Maple leaves on the sandstone bluff, Upper Buffalo Wilderness, Ozark National Forest

Umbrella magnolia blossom (double exposure blur), Buffalo River Wilderness

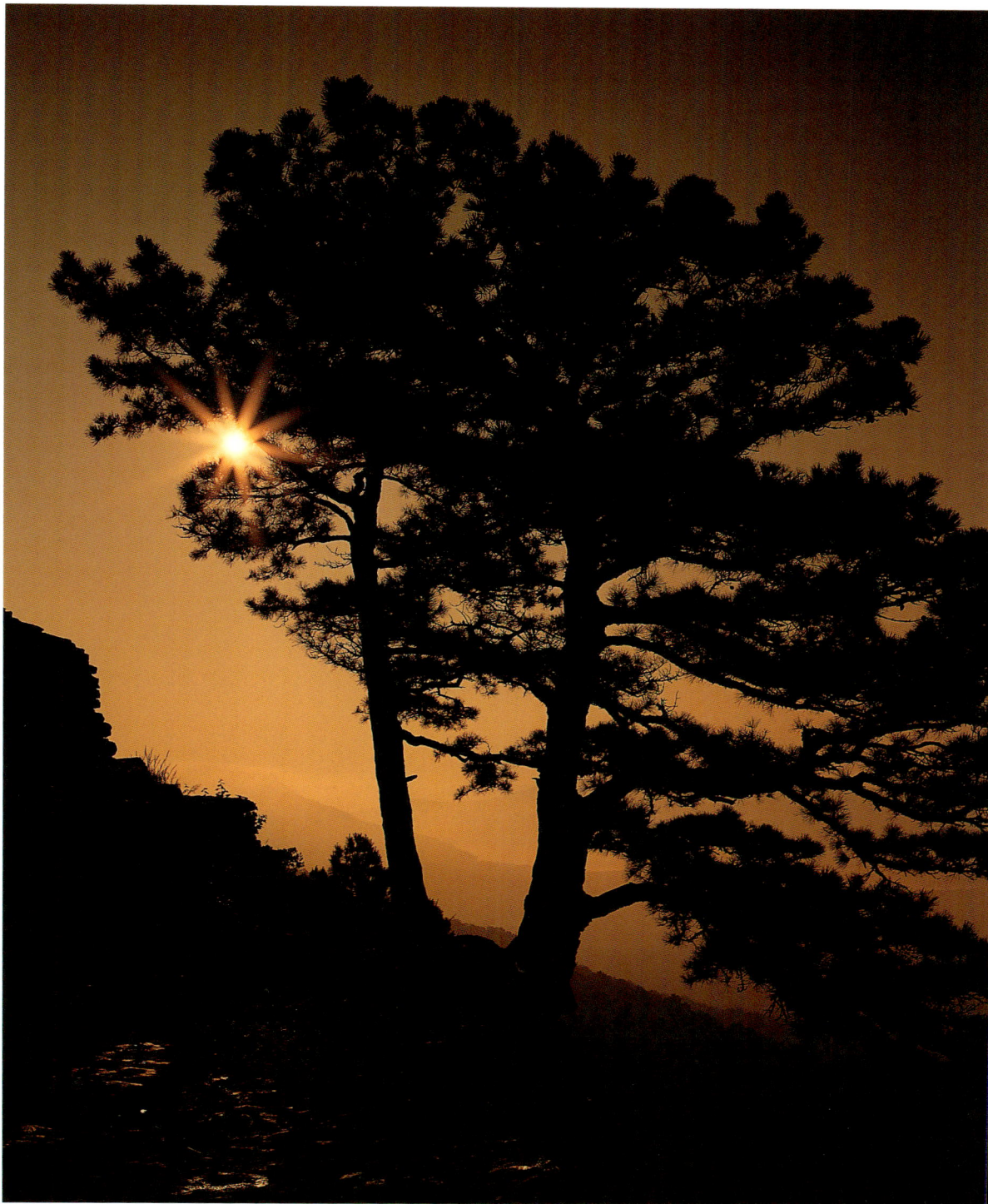

Sunrise, shortleaf pine, from Scenic 7 National Scenic Byway

Star trails w/North Star (four-hour exposure), Pedestal Rocks Scenic Area, Ozark National Forest

Whitetail deer fawn along the Ozark Highlands Trail, Ozark National Forest

◄ *The star "trails" in this photo are made possible because the earth rotates—if you leave your camera's shutter open long enough, the stars will gradually move across the sky and make these "trails." If you look close, you will see many different colors produced by the various gases of the stars burning. It was completely dark when I made this photo—the pedestal rock was lit by a strobe light that I fired off during the exposure. While sitting there in the darkness waiting for the stars to move, a bear came up behind me to see what I was up to—yikes!*

Redbud blossoms and moss,
Broadwater Hollow, Buffalo National River

Details, details, the beauty is in the details! Anyone who has gone into the field with me for a photo trip knows that I spend a lot of time down on my hands and knees. I teach—no, make that PREACH—macro photography in my photo workshops. There is so much beauty in life that we all pass right on by without noticing, if only we would take the time to stop and look around. Heck, look right down at our own feet!

I have found that carpets of moss are often used by Momma Nature as her canvas, and that she tosses all sorts of normal stuff down onto that canvas to create delightful art. I particularly like the times of the year when she drops colorful things out of the trees—especially in the spring or fall.

Cloudy, misty days bring out all the rich colors of moss. The air was saturated and ready to dump on me while I was taking this photo. In fact, the rain began before I was finished, and I had to use an umbrella that I always carry in my camera bag to shield the camera. When it rains I don't put away the camera—I pack more film!

◄ Fall reflections in a backwater swamp, St. Francis National Forest

The forest floor in October, Ozark National Forest

Every photographer wants to see their work on the cover of a magazine. This photograph was my first ever magazine cover, appearing on the cover of Arkansas Times *magazine. Since then it has been published in numerous books, magazines, posters, and brochures, and it has been printed with at least FIVE different orientations, depending on how the editor wanted to use it. It has even been published backwards and upside down a couple of times. Some images look silly when printed incorrectly, while others—like this one—work fine no matter how you look at them.*

➤ Eden Falls at Lost Valley, Buffalo National River

Sunset over Beaver Lake

◄ Sandstone boulder and lichens, Forked Mountain, Flatside Wilderness, Ouachita National Forest

This rock is located high atop Forked Mountain, one of the most unique mountains in Arkansas. I first saw this mountain while hiking the Ouachita Trail back in the late 1970's. Not knowing any other way to get there, I bushwhacked with 50 pounds of camera gear for many hours up and down hills and through thick brush, finally arriving at the base of the mountain. After a 30-minute climb up an incredible boulder field, I made it to the top. The view from up there is quite spectacular, but my favorite photo from that trip is of this rock covered with lichens. Now I know there is a road that goes almost all the way to the top! (That final 30 minutes UP is still quite a climb.)

Sandstone and water, Kings River Natural Area

Maple tree caught in the snow, Buffalo National River

Maple forest (double exposure blur), Upper Buffalo Wilderness, Ozark National Forest

Mayapple meets the rising sun, Ozarks

The trail to Hemmed-In Hollow after a late-season snowfall, Ponca Wilderness, Buffalo National River

This is the trail that leads down into Hemmed-In Hollow, and it was covered with 14 inches of new snow when I arrived. My entire focus for the day was to get some good images of the big waterfall there. The process of just getting to that falls became my main goal. I had my trusty cross-country skis, and enjoyed some really nice moments of quiet bliss moving through the wilderness. But the trail quickly became very steep, and nearly impossible to ski for a novice like me (I bit the dust in a spectacular fall more than once!). I ended up removing my skis and struggling on down through the heavy snow on foot.

One of the images that I shot that day of the thundering waterfall appears on page 16 in this book, and remains one of my all-time favorite and most successful photographs. But I am really glad that I stopped and made the effort to record this scene at right, especially before I messed it all up with my skis. It is a very happy, tranquil scene to me, one that shows the beauty of the ordinary, in the soft blanket of new-fallen snow, and the graceful lines and curves and colors of the shadows. Those very same skis hang on the wall of our log cabin, and each time I see this image, I give a nod to the skis, and tell them, and myself, that it will snow again.

Often times the journey is as good or better than the destination!

◄ Purple coneflowers (*Echinacea*), Leatherwood Wilderness, Ozark National Forest

Sunrise from Brush Heap Mountain, Athens-Big Fork Trail, Ouachita National Forest

The trail to reach this viewpoint is one of the steepest in the entire state—actually it's an old mule trail mail route from the 1800's. It was a hot, muggy and buggy July morning when I hiked up the trail in the dark to capture this sunrise. The effort was well worth it though—this is one of my most published photographs of all time. Besides appearing in many book and magazine articles, it was used one year by the Arkansas Tourism department as the main photo in their national ad campaign to sell the beauty of Arkansas. It has appeared in hundreds of publications.

Dancing willows in the early morning fog, Shores Lake, Ozark National Forest

Jessica and her dog, Hawksbill Crag, Upper Buffalo Wilderness, Ozark National Forest

Dogwood and moss, Richland Creek Wilderness, Ozark National Forest

Hemmed-In Hollow Falls, Ponca Wilderness, Buffalo National River

Maple trees reaching for the sky, Ozarks

Cossatot River, Cossatot River State Park Natural Area

Elk grazing in Boxley Valley, Buffalo National River

Sandstone boulder and cascade, Boen Gulf drainage, Upper Buffalo Wilderness, Ozark National Forest

There are three magnificent waterfalls in an upper canyon of the Boen Gulf drainage that I have hiked in to photograph many times. Each time I go in I pass by this neat little cascade. I usually dismiss it as just a minor beauty spot, yet the cascade seems to always be flowing, and the moss lush and green, no matter how dry and unimpressive the other waterfalls are. I have never picked this photo for publication before, but I always keep it in my "A" pile of slides, hoping to find a place to use it. I think that life is like that in many ways for us humans, too—some of us may not be the biggest or the brightest, but we hang in there anyway, waiting for our chance to shine. This little cascade has no name, but it has risen to the surface, and is my favorite photo from Boen Gulf.

◄ October reflections in the Buffalo River near Erbie

Sunrise from Scenic 7 National Scenic Byway

➤ *I spend a lot of time listening to what others say about my photographs. Sometimes the ones I think are just wonderful fall flat, while others that I hadn't paid too much attention to, people rave about. That has been the case with this image taken along Caney Creek—lots of folks love it. I think the reason this image works is that the stream grabs you right up front, leads you past a little hillside of wildflowers, under a bluff, and off into the wilderness. I guess that is what I hope to accomplish with each photograph that I take—I want to draw the viewer up into the scene, to a beautiful place to get away to for a few moments. This particular image takes me back to that steep and rough hillside covered with wildflowers, and how I struggled to keep from sliding down it while I found a steady platform for my tripod (I cut my leg on a sharp rock in the process, washing the blood off in the cool stream). It was a long, hard day, but I'm a happy camper if others can take pleasure from what I produce.*

Fire pink and phlox, Caney Creek Wilderness, Ouachita National Forest

November reflections, Caney Creek Wilderness, Ouachita National Forest

◄ Neil Compton's Double Falls, Whitaker Creek, Upper Buffalo Wilderness, Ozark National Forest

Deciduous holly and moss, Richland Creek Valley, Ozark National Forest

January frost in the hardwoods, White Rock Mountain, Ozark National Forest

Triple Falls at Camp Orr, Buffalo National River

Cedar tree, south rim of Mt. Magazine, Mt. Magazine State Park

This book is for the butterfly lady—
She gave me life.
She taught me by example to protect and cherish the natural world around us.
And she encouraged me to make my own trails.
Thanks Mom!

◄ Eastern tiger swallowtail butterfly and dogwood, Sweden Creek Natural Area

I caught this butterfly on film quite by accident. It was a windy day, and I was trying to get
a nice photo of these beautiful dogwood blossoms, but needed the wind to stop com-
pletely before I could take any pictures. So I stood there behind my tripod, with my hand
on the cable release, waiting for the right moment. Just when the wind decided to cooper-
ate, this friendly butterfly landed on the blooms right in front of my camera!

My Mom absolutely loved butterflies. She passed away shortly before I took this
picture, and I bet this yellow jewel was her way of sending good cheer on down to me.
I think of her now every time that I see a butterfly.

Photography Notes

It has been nearly 30 years since I first picked up a camera and headed out into the forest. Since then I have gone through six completely different camera systems. I started off with Nikon F2 & F3 35mm outfits, then went to a Zone VI 4/5 large format camera, then down to a Leica R6 35mm, up to medium format with a Pentax 6/7, back down again to 35mm with a Contax RTS III, and finally up to a Contax 645 medium format. Each system had its advantages, and photographs taken with them all are included in this book. See the following two pages for details.

My film of choice for many years now has been Fuji Velvia slide film. It is the only film I have ever used that seems to match the color, sharpness and "feel" of the scenes that I photograph. Before Velvia there was Kodachrome, and I've even shot a lot of Ektachrome in the large-format days. The slower the film speed, the sharper and better quality the images are, so my films have always had a very slow speed, all the way down to 25.

This is perhaps the last picture book that I will produce from traditional film camera equipment. Digital is quickly becoming the standard of the industry, and I welcome it with open arms. In the years to come we will all be shooting digital. One of the many advantages of digital is the fact that you can do quite a bit of manipulation to the images in the computer and still retain a realistic-looking image. I have not gotten into any of that yet, and what you see on these pages is what came out of the camera—there is no computer manipulation at all. Another great advantage to digital media is that once you buy the memory disks, all of your "film" is FREE—no more film to buy, or processing bills! I've been known to shoot a hundred or more photos of a single scene, and the film and processing costs really add up fast.

My favorite lenses are wide angles (in the 20mm–24mm range) and macros. I like the different perspectives of the world that these lenses produce. Using a macro also forces me to slow the pace a bit, get down on my hands and knees, and examine the details on the forest floor—you tend to see and enjoy a lot more of the natural world that way.

I don't use many filters or other gadgets. I do use a polarizing filter, especially on overcast and misty days, when it really reduces glare in the atmosphere and makes the colors pop. A heavy tripod is standard, and my "backpacking" model weighs 12 pounds. The total weight of my camera gear is normally around 40 pounds. Digital equipment will weigh less than TEN!

There are a couple of techniques I use that always draw questions. We spend a lot of time on these during my photo workshops. The first one is used on waterfalls and fast-moving streams and produces that silky, dreamy effect. All you do is use a slow shutter speed—something a full second or longer. The second effect is what I call "double exposure blur," and is noted on several images in this book. It requires a simple double exposure, with one exposure being in focus, and the other being completely out of focus. It's easy, and fun, and you never know what you are going to come up with.

Being a wilderness photographer often means getting up in the middle of the night and hiking in the darkness for miles, crossing flooded streams, being eaten alive by bugs and other critters, and many long hours and days and weeks of sweat and toil, year after year. But I have no boss, and I rather love it. I suspect I'll keep it up for another 30 years.

Illustrations List

All of the images were taken on Fuji Velvia film (unless otherwise noted)

Page #	Camera and lens	Page #	Camera and lens
66–67	Pentax 6/7, 75mm lens, polarizer	100	Contax RTS III, 28mm lens, polarizer, double exposure blur
69	Contax 645, 120mm macro lens, warm polarizer	101	Contax 645, 120mm macro lens, warm polarizer
70	Contax RTS II, 28mm zoom lens	102–103	Contax RTS III, 100 macro lens, polarizer
71	Contax 645, 120mm macro lens, warm polarizer	105	Pentax 6/7, 135mm lens, polarizer
72	Pentax 6/7, 135mm macro lens, polarizer	106	Zone VI 4/5, 210mm lens, Cokin P 198 filter (Fuji 100)
73	Contax 645, 120mm macro lens, warm polarizer	107	Nikon F2, 105mm lens (Kodachrome 25)
74	Contax RTS III, 100mm macro, polarizer, frozen tush	108	Contax RTS III, 60mm zoom lens
75	Contax 645, 120mm macro lens, warm polarizer	109	Contax 645, 120mm macro lens, warm polarizer
76	Contax RTS III, 21mm lens (lens flare no extra charge)	110	Contax RTS III, 200mm zoom lens, polarizer
77	Zone VI 4/5, 210mm lens (Fuji 50)	111	Pentax 6/7, 45mm lens, polarizer
78–79	Contax 645, 120mm macro lens, warm polarizer	112	Zone VI 4/5, 120mm lens, polarizer (Fuji 100)
81	Pentax 6/7, 35mm fish-eye lens	113	Contax RTS III, 300mm zoom lens, polarizer
82	Contax RTS III, 100mm macro lens, polarizer	114–115	Contax RTS III, 40mm zoom lens
83	Zone VI 4/5, 210mm lens, polarizer (Ektachrome 100)	117	Contax RTS III, 28mm zoom lens, polarizer
84	Contax RTS III, 55mm zoom lens, polarizer	118	Pentax 6/7, 300mm lens
85	Contax RTS III, 21mm lens, polarizer	119	Pentax 6/7, 75mm lens, polarizer (Kodak Lumiere X)
86	Contax RTS III, 100mm macro lens, polarizer, double exposure blur	120	Contax 645, 45mm lens, warm polarizer
87	Zone VI 4/5, 210mm lens, Cokin P 198 filter (Fuji 50)	121	Pentax 6/7, 135mm lens
88	Pentax 6/7, 75mm lens (4 hour exposure, with flash)	122	Contax RTS III, 100 macro lens, polarizer
89	Nikon F2, 20mm lens (Kodachrome 64)	123	Nikon F2, 24mm lens, polarizer (Kodachrome 64)
90–91	Leica R6, 28mm lens	124	Contax RTS III, 40mm zoom lens, warm polarizer
93	Contax 645, 120mm macro lens, warm polarizer	125	Pentax 6/7, 75mm lens, polarizer, Cokin P 198 filter
94	Nikon F2, 55mm macro lens (Kodachrome 64)	126–127	Contax RTS II, 40mm zoom lens, warm polarizer
95	Pentax 6/7, 105mm lens (Kodak Lumiere)	132	Contax RTS III, 80mm zoom lens, polarizer
96	Zone VI 4/5, 210mm lens, polarizer (Ektachrome 100)	Front Cover	Zone VI 4/5, 210mm lens, Cokin P 198 filter (Fuji 100)
97	Nikon F3, 60mm macro lens		
98	Contax 645, 120mm macro lens, warm polarizer	Back Cover	Contax 645, 120mm macro lens, warm polarizer
99	Pentax 6/7, 135mm macro lens, polarizer		

Redbud Falls, Ozarks

This photograph was taken in the middle of the day with the sun shining—normally the worst conditions for good nature photography. But it has graced the covers of many publications, and is one of my favorite images of all time, so I guess it turned out OK after all.

I love contrasts in nature: here you have the dark hardness of the sandstone bluff; the bright, fluid waterfall spray; and the delicate, colorful flowers of the redbud tree.

An ice storm took down this tree several years ago, so this scene cannot be repeated—at least, in this same location. While doing research for my <u>Arkansas Waterfalls Guidebook</u> *I found many great waterfalls that had redbud trees growing at their bases and up the sides, some with dogwoods, too. So now when folks ask me how to find this scene, I tell them to pick up a copy of the guidebook and take lots of film!*